# AURAL TEST SURVIVAL BOOK

## Grade 3

## Caroline Evans

LONDON • FRANKFURT/M • LEIPZIG • NEW YORK
www.editionpeters.com

3 95

Peters Edition Limited
2-6 Baches Street
London
N1 6DN
England

Tel: +44 (0)20 7553 4000
Fax: +44 (0)20 7490 4921
e-mail: sales@editionpeters.com
Internet: www.editionpeters.com

First published 2006
Revised edition published 2012

ISBN 978-1-84367-042-1

A catalogue record for this book is available from the British Library

Cover design: www.adamhaystudio.com

Illustrations: Joy FitzSimmons

Printed in the UK by Halstan & Co Ltd, Amersham, Bucks.

# CONTENTS

The *Aural Test Survival Book* offers a chapter-by-chapter look at responses to questions typically asked by examiners. The speed and accuracy of your responses will help you gain a better mark.

About the *Aural Test Survival Book* ..... page 4

Clap in time ............................... page 5
  . . . when the examiner says: *"First, clap in time while I play. Join in as soon as you can and give a louder clap on the strong beats . . . Is it in two time, three time or four time?"*

Sing echoes ................................ page 11
  . . . when the examiner says: *"Next I'd like you to sing three phrases as echoes. Here is the key-chord . . . . and your starting note . . ."*

Spot the difference ....................... page 17
  . . . when the examiner says: *"Now I'll play a phrase twice, but with a change in either pitch or rhythm the second time. Tell me what the difference was. Here is the key-chord . . . and the tonic . . . And now with the change . . . How was it different?"*

Describe the music ........................ page 25
  . . . when the examiner says: *"Listen to this piece, then I'll ask you about . . . and about major or minor key . . ."*

Find out the meaning ..................... page 32
  . . . a list of musical terms and their meanings

## Key to Symbols

**T** Time

**R** Rhythm

**K** Key

# About ... the Aural Test Survival Book

Don't be scared of aural tests! The *Aural Test Survival Book* will help you improve your listening skills and prepare you for the aural test in your music exam. You can use this book with a teacher, parent or friend, or you can practise the exercises on your own.

This book will encourage you to listen to music more actively and give you confidence to tackle the aural tests in your exam.

Try to spend a little time on aural skills as part of your regular practice. You already have your examination pieces, studies and scales. Now here's your own book of aural skills!

*Caroline Evans*

## A note to teachers

The material in the *Aural Test Survival Book* corresponds to the Associated Board's aural requirements for music examinations and is suitable for all instrumentalists. Many of the tests are common to other examination boards and so students preparing for any music exam will find the book useful.

You can try out the activities in your lessons, or you can set them for your students to complete at home. The format of the book encourages students to think in terms of three important elements of music: Time, Rhythm and Key.

# CLAP IN TIME

## When the examiner says:

*"First, clap in time while I play. Join in as soon as you can and give a louder clap on the strong beats . . . Is it in two time, three time or four time?"*

## What should you do?

Clap the beat of a short piece of music in 2- (2/4, 2/2 or 6/8), 3- (3/4, 3/8 or 9/8) or 4-time (4/4).

When the music starts, join in as soon as possible, clapping the beat.

Clap louder on the strong beats.

You will then be asked to state the time: 2-time, 3-time or 4-time. In other words, say whether there are 2, 3 or 4 beats in a bar. You do not need to state the full time signature.

## What you need to know

BEAT is regular, like a clock ticking. RHYTHM is the varying note lengths and patterns within each beat. Rhythm varies; the beat is regular. Make sure you clap the beat rather than the rhythm.

6/8 TIME is in 2-time. You may hear groups of three quavers in the music and think the music is in 3-time. In fact each group of three quavers is played in the time of ONE dotted crotchet beat.

There are therefore TWO dotted crotchet beats in a bar. This is called compound time:

9/8 TIME is in 3-time. There are THREE dotted crotchet beats in a bar.

The music will not necessarily start on the first beat of the bar.

## How should you do it?

### Before the music starts:

- Put your hands in position, ready to start clapping.

### While listening:

- It may help to sway your body in time with the beat. Even better, tap your toe gently.
- Start counting in your head.
- Listen for the strong beats. These are usually on the first beat of the bar and will be slightly accented.
- Decide how many beats are in a bar.

### When you start clapping:

- Clap the beat in time with the examiner. Don't clap the rhythm.
- Start clapping with the music as soon as you can.
- Clap loudly on the strong beats and lightly on the weaker beats.
- When you have finished clapping, state whether there are 2, 3 or 4 beats in a bar.

- **Stand tall**
- **Sound confident**
- **Speak out**

## Music in 2-time

You may know the song *Oh dear, what can the matter be*. Sing it to yourself and march round the room in time. Stamp your foot on the strong beats. If you can't remember this song, here are its opening rhythms and words:

Now look at the rhythms again. Clap the beat, NOT the rhythm. The strong beats are marked with accents (>). Clap louder on the strong beats:

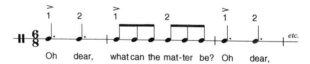

Now try counting three beats in a bar (1-2-3-1-2-3) to this song; can you feel how the music doesn't fit?

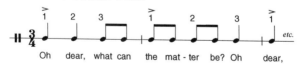

Finally, clap the beat in 2-time once more. Remember to clap louder on the strong beats. If you know the tune, sing it at the same time.

## Music in 3-time

If the music is in 3-time you won't be able to march to it (try marching to a tune in 3-time and see how the strong beat keeps falling on the opposite foot). Here are the rhythms and words of *Away in a manger*, which is in simple triple time (3/4):

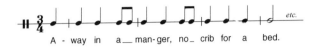

A - way in    a___ man- ger, no_ crib for a    bed.

Now look at the rhythms again and clap the beat (not the rhythm). Clap louder on the strong beats – they are marked with accents (>):

A - way in    a___ man- ger, no_ crib for a    bed.

Now try counting two beats in a bar to *Away in a manger*. Can you feel how the music doesn't fit?

A - way in    a___ man- ger, no_ crib for    a bed.

9/8 is also 3-time. In 9/8, the beat is a dotted crotchet – you will hear flowing quavers with each bar containing three groups of three quavers. You can see this rhythm in the country dance called *Sir Roger de Coverley*:

## Music in 4-time

Just like music in 2-time, you will find you can march to music in 4-time. It's sometimes difficult to tell whether music is in 2-time or 4-time. It often depends on the speed and character of the piece. These hints will help:

- Listen carefully for the strong beats. The beat at the beginning of the bar is stressed more than the weaker beats, so 4/4 will be 1-2-3-4-1-2-3-4 while 2/4 will be 1-2-1-2.

- There is often a stress on the third beat in 4-time but it is not as strong as the first beat.

- A piece in 2-time often sounds quite bright and brisk. It won't be wrong if you say 2-time instead of 4-time but the examiner might query your answer by asking if you are sure.

Here are the rhythms and words of *John Brown's body*. Sing it and march round the room in time.

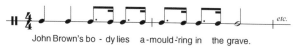

John Brown's bo - dy lies  a -mould-'ring in  the grave.

Now look at the rhythms again and clap the beat (not the rhythm). Clap louder on the strong beats – they are marked with accents (>):

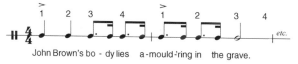

John Brown's bo - dy lies  a -mould-'ring in  the grave.

## How to improve further

Every time you hear any music on the TV, radio, CD or mp3 player, clap the beat, or tap your toe. Try and work out how many beats there are in a bar.

## The aim of the test

This test is designed to help you play your own pieces rhythmically and in time.

## Quiz

Are the following in 2-time, 3-time or 4-time?

1. The *Can-Can*, by Offenbach.

2. The theme tune to *EastEnders*.

Answers on page 32.

1. Be sure to clap the beat, NOT the rhythm.

2. When you clap, be precise. Keep one hand still, palm upwards, and clap your other hand against it.

3. The strong beats will be slightly accented. Clap louder on the strong beats than on the weaker beats.

4. Work out whether the music is in 2-, 3- or 4-time before the examiner asks you; start counting the beats in your head as soon as the music starts.

5. Don't try to work out the number of beats in a bar by counting the length of the last note – it may be followed by a rest.

## Clap in Time:

**T** Time: clap in time with the beat as soon as you can. Count the number of beats in a bar and state the time

**R** Rhythm: be aware of how the rhythm fits with the beat, but be sure to clap the beat, not the rhythm

# SING ECHOES

## When the examiner says:

*"Next I'd like you to sing three phrases as echoes. Here is the key-chord . . . and your starting note . . ."*

## What should you do?

Sing, as "echoes", three short phrases played by the examiner. If you prefer, you may hum or whistle.

After each phrase is played, sing exactly what you have just heard played on the piano, immediately following on and in time with the beat.

Concentrate on the rhythm as well as the tune.

## What you need to know

The three phrases will be two bars long, in a major or minor key, and will cover no more than an octave. They will begin on the tonic, third or fifth note of the scale. These notes are contained in the key-chord which is played at the start.

The examiner will always begin by playing the key-chord and the starting note, and will give a count-in of two bars (for example: 1-2-3-1-2-3).

After the examiner has played each phrase, you should sing back as an echo "in time". This means you should keep in time with the speed started on the piano. Do not hesitate before you start.

## How should you do it?

### While listening:

- As soon as the examiner gives the count-in, gently tap your toe in time, right through to the end of the test.

- Listen carefully to the rhythm as well as the tune – the rhythm is just as important.

- Listen to the key-chord and starting note (tonic), and keep them in mind throughout the test.

### When you start singing:

- Keep tapping your toe gently in time while singing the echo.

- Sing "lah" to each note. If you prefer, you may hum or whistle, although it is very hard to whistle accurately.

- Don't pause after the examiner has finished playing – come straight in and keep to the same speed as the examiner, particularly when the phrase ends on a long note.

- Keep the key-chord in your mind – your starting note will be one of the notes in the chord.

- If you hear *staccato* (detached) notes, sing short notes.

- Don't cut short any notes that are long.

## At all times:

- **Stand tall**
- **Sound confident**
- **Sing out**

## Training session

Often your response to this test will be automatic. But here are a few steps to help sing back a tune accurately.

Play some major and minor scales on your own instrument (if voice is your instrument, then sing). Play at a comfortable speed and tap your toe gently to keep in time. Here are D major (ascending) and C melodic minor (descending):

If you play a bass-clef instrument, here are the same scales in the bass clef:

When you have played each scale, sing it. In order for it to be comfortable for your voice, you may need to sing it an octave higher or lower than you played it.

Keep to the same speed you played before, and still tap your toe gently to keep in time. Sing "lah" or "doh" to each note, and make sure each note is separated.

As you sing, try to see the shape of the music in your head. It may help to draw the shape in the air with your hand. For example, if you play an ascending and descending scale, it will look like this:

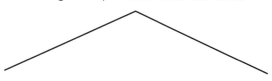

# Test 3B

Look at the following music. The notes are the same as those in the major scale you have just played and sung:

Start by clapping the rhythms of the notes printed, filling in the gaps by repeating (in other words, echoing) the printed rhythms. Don't leave a gap before your echo – keep to the same speed:

Now play the notes on your instrument, singing the echoes in the gaps. Remember to keep to the same speed. Play the notes of the key-chord first.

If you play a bass-clef instrument, here is the same music in the bass clef:

Now look at the following music. The notes used are the same as the minor scale on page 13. First clap the rhythm, clapping echoes in the gaps. Then play the music on your instrument, singing the echoes. Count yourself in before you start to play.

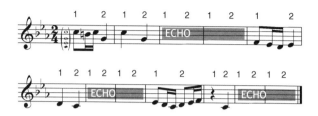

Here is the same music in the bass clef:

## How to improve further

Play the first two bars of a piece you are learning and sing them back. Then do the same for two other bars in the same piece.

Listen to some music you don't know and practise singing back short phrases. You could use the radio or TV and press the mute button while you sing echoes.

## The aim of the test

This test is designed to develop your melodic memory.

## Quiz

Draw the shape (either on paper or in the air with your hand) of the opening bars of the following songs. Answers on page 32.

1. *Ode to Joy* by Beethoven

2. *Auld Lang Syne*

1. Don't worry about the sound of your voice; concentrate on singing in tune and in time.

2. Even if you feel nervous, try to *appear* confident. Sing out – a loud mistake is better than a quiet one.

3. Take a breath before you sing so that you don't run out of air on the long notes.

4. Use bright vowels – "lah" is usually best.

5. Don't "swoop" up or down to the next note.

6. If you hear *staccato* notes, sing short notes.

7. It may help to follow the shape of the phrase with your hand as you listen and sing.

8. Sing *something*, even if you're unsure – just get the rhythm right and end on the tonic.

## Follow the TRaK:

**T** Time: tap your toe in time with the beat while listening and singing

**R** Rhythm: listen carefully to the rhythm as well as the tune and don't cut long notes short

**K** Key: listen carefully to the key-chord and starting note so that you sing in tune

## When the examiner says:

*"Now I'll play a phrase twice, but with a change in either pitch or rhythm the second time. Tell me what the difference was. Here is the key-chord . . . and the tonic . . . And now with the change . . . How was it different?"*

## What should you do?

Spot the difference in pitch or rhythm of a four-bar phrase played twice.

Clap, sing or describe the difference.

## What you need to know

The examiner will play the key-chord and tonic note and give a count-in of two bars (for example, 1-2-3-1-2-3) before playing the first version.

A four-bar phrase will be played twice, with a change in the second playing.

There will be just one change, either to the pitch (one note will be higher or lower) or to the rhythm (one note will be longer or shorter).

Both versions will be played a second time if necessary, although this will affect your mark.

## How should you do it?

### While listening:

- Pick up the beat as soon as it is indicated by tapping your toe gently. This will help you to follow the music.

- Decide *what*: is the change to the pitch or rhythm?
  Decide *where*: is the change at the beginning, middle or end?
  Decide *how*: is the changed note higher or lower, longer or shorter?

## When you answer:

- Either clap the difference, sing the difference, or raise your hand when you hear the difference and then explain it.

- If you clap or sing the difference, clap or sing the second version.

- Keep tapping the beat gently with your toe right through to the end of the test.

- Answer straight away.

## At all times:

- **Stand tall**
- **Sound confident**
- **Speak/sing out**

## Training session

If you haven't done grade 2 aural tests, start by looking at this test in grade 2, where the music phrases are shorter.

### Pitch changes

The second version of the phrase may contain a change of pitch. In other words, one of the notes will be higher or lower. Only one note will be altered.

Play this short phrase on your instrument. As before, choose a comfortable speed and gently tap crotchets with your toe.

If you play a bass-clef instrument, here is a version in the bass clef:

Keep tapping your toe gently and play this slightly different version.

Here is a bass-clef version:

The rhythms are exactly the same in both phrases, but one note pitch is different. Can you describe the difference? It may help if you sing the two versions. Keep tapping the crotchet beat with your toe.

You should hear a difference in the middle of the phrase. If you describe the difference in words, you might say:

*"There was a higher note in the middle of the phrase."*

While the music is playing, you can raise your hand to show where the difference is, and then describe the difference.

If you answer by saying and singing:

*"The notes in the middle of the phrase went ♩♩"*

Now play these two phrases. Once again, before you start, tap a steady beat with your toe.

# Test 3C

Here are the same phrases in the bass clef:

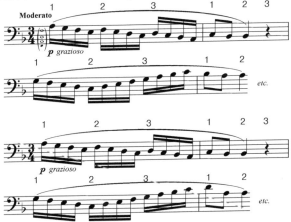

This time you should hear a difference near the end. Sing the two versions and listen carefully to the tune.

If you describe the difference in words, you might say:

*"There was a pitch change. In the second version, there was a higher note near the end."*

If you answer by saying and singing:

*"There was a pitch change. In the second version the note near the end went higher, like this ♪♪♪♪♪♪♪"*

## Rhythmic changes

The second version may contain a change to the rhythm instead.

Play this short phrase on your instrument. Before you start, choose a comfortable speed and gently tap crotchets with your toe. Listen carefully to the rhythm while you play.

F. Gruber

If you play a bass-clef instrument, here is a version an octave lower and in the bass clef:

Keep tapping your toe gently and play this slightly different version:

Here is a bass-clef version:

The note names are the same in both phrases, but the rhythms are slightly different. Can you describe the difference? It may help if you clap the rhythms of the two versions first. Keep tapping the crotchet beat with your toe.

You should hear a difference in the second bar. If you describe the difference in words, you might say:

*"In the second version the notes near the beginning were even".*

While the music is playing, you can raise your hand to show where the difference is, and then describe the difference.

If you answer by saying and clapping:

*"In the second version, the notes near the beginning went ♪♪♪♩. ".*

Now play these two phrases. Once again, before you start, tap a steady beat with your toe.

Here are the same phrases in the bass clef:

This time you should hear a difference right at the start of the phrase. Clap the two versions and listen carefully to the rhythms.

If you describe the difference in words, you might say:

*"There was a rhythmic change. In the second version, the first note was shorter."*

You can raise your hand while the music is playing, to show where the difference is, before describing it.

If you answer by saying and clapping:

*"There was a rhythmic change. In the second version, the first two notes went like this - ♫ ♩ "*

Now play the two phrases on the following page and describe both the pitch change and the rhythmic change – out loud. As usual, before you start, tap a steady beat with your toe. It may help if you clap the rhythms first.

Here are the same phrases in the bass clef:

## How to improve further

*Play* the first four bars of your favourite pieces. Play them again and make a mistake, altering the pitch. Only change the pitch of one note. Put into words or sing what you have done.

*Clap* the first four bars of the pieces you are playing at the moment. When you clap them a second time, make a mistake and alter the rhythm. Then describe it – out loud.

Reading and playing the music yourself will help you describe the pitch and rhythmic changes.

## The aim of the test

The purpose of this test is to help you become more aware of pitch and rhythm when listening.

1. You may find that closing your eyes helps you to concentrate.

2. Start tapping your toe in time when the examiner gives the count-in, and keep tapping continuously throughout both versions of the phrase.

3. Remember to think: *what* (pitch or rhythmic change), *where* (beginning, middle or end), *how* (higher/lower or longer/shorter).

4. Sometimes it can be hard to describe the difference. If so, try to clap or sing to show what you mean.

5. If you can't spot the difference the first time don't be afraid to ask the examiner to play the phrases again, although this will affect your mark.

## Follow the TRaK:

**T** Time: tap your toe in time with the beat as soon as the examiner indicates it, and keep tapping steadily throughout the test

**R** Rhythm: decide if it is the pitch or the rhythm which changes in the second playing

**K** Key: listen to the key-chord. If you sing the difference, sing in tune

# DESCRIBE THE MUSIC

## When the examiner says:

*"Listen to this piece, then I'll ask you about . . . and about major or minor key . . . "*

## What should you do?

The examiner will play a short piece of music and then ask you one or two short questions about two features. The first feature will be one of the following:

**Loud or quiet**
(sometimes described as dynamics)

**Gradually getting louder or quieter**

**Detached or smooth**
(sometimes described as articulation)

**Becoming faster or slower**
(sometimes described as tempo)

The second feature will be:

**Major or minor**
(sometimes described as tonality)

## What you need to know

You should try to know the meaning of the following Italian words. But if you can't remember the Italian word, use the English.

**Loud or quiet (dynamics)**

**loud**
Italian: *forte*
symbol: $f$

**quiet**
Italian: *piano*
symbol: $p$

## Gradually getting louder or quieter

### gradually getting louder
Italian: *crescendo*
symbol: ————— (an "opening hairpin")

### gradually getting quieter
Italian: *diminuendo*
symbol: ════—— (a "closing hairpin")

## Detached or smooth (articulation)

### detached
Italian: *staccato*
symbol: ♪ ♩

### smooth
Italian: *legato*
symbol: ⌒ (a slur)

## Faster or slower (tempo)

### gradually getting faster
Italian: *accelerando* (*accel.*) or *stringendo*

### gradually getting slower
Italian: *rallentando* (*rall.*) or *ritardando*
(*ritard.*)

## How should you do it?

## Before the music starts:

- You only need to listen for two features; the examiner will tell you which BEFORE the music starts.

## While listening:

- Concentrate only on the particular musical features specified.

## When you answer:

- State even what seems obvious.

- Try to use Italian words like *accelerando, rallentando, forte, piano, crescendo, diminuendo, staccato* and *legato* in your answers, but using English words is acceptable.

## At all times:

- **Stand tall**
- **Sound confident**
- **Speak out**

## Training session

The following piece of music uses the notes of the key-chord of D major. Play it on your instrument, or sing it.

Here it is an octave lower and in the bass clef:

Now play it with contrasted dynamics:

Answer this question about what you have just played:
*"The piece started loudly. Where was the quietest point in the music? Did it gradually or suddenly become quiet?"*

Now play it with *legato* and *staccato* notes:

## Test 3D

Answer this question:
*"The piece started with smooth notes.
Were the notes in the second half of the
piece smooth or detached?"*

Now vary the speed of your playing:

Answer this question about what you have
just played:
*"Did the tempo stay the same throughout
the piece?"*

The piece you have just been playing is in
a major key. Now play this version, which
is in a minor key. Watch out for the key
signature:

When you change from a major to a minor
key, one note in the key-chord changes.
Which one is it?

Listen to some music on the radio or on
a CD. Think about the different ways you
have just played and decide whether the
music you are listening to is:

> loud (*forte*) or quiet (*piano*)

> getting gradually louder (*crescendo*)
> or gradually quieter (*diminuendo*)

> detached (*staccato*) or smooth
> (*legato*)

getting gradually faster (*accelerando*) or gradually slower (*rallentando*)

in a major or minor key

Practise saying the answers out loud even if you are on your own. This is important because saying the answer is very different from thinking about the answer.

Here are some examples of questions you might be asked, and the sort of words you could use to answer them:

## Loud or quiet

*Question*: "Where was the loudest point in the music?"

*Answer*: "It was loudest at the end."

*Question*: "Was the change from quiet to loud sudden or gradual?"

*Answer*: "Gradual: there was a *crescendo*."

## Detached or smooth

*Question*: "Was the beginning played smoothly or was it detached?"

*Answer*: "It was played smoothly, or *legato*."

*Question*: "Were the loud chords smooth or detached?"

*Answer*: "They were detached, or *staccato*."

## Faster or slower

*Question*: "Did the speed of the music change at all, or did it always stay the same?"

*Answer*: "It slowed down a little towards the end (there was a *rallentando*)."

*Question*: "Was there any change in the speed of the music, or did it always stay the same?"

*Answer*: "It gradually got faster towards the end: there was an *accelerando*".

**Major or minor**

*Question*: "Did the piece end in a major or a minor key?"

*Answer*: "It ended in a minor key."

## How to improve further

Every time you hear any music try to follow the journey it takes. Choose a musical feature – loud/quiet, detached/smooth, faster/slower, major/minor, – and see if you can describe it.

Say the answers out loud even if you are on your own – thinking you are able to answer the questions is often rather different from actually answering them.

## The aim of the test

This test is designed to encourage you to *listen* to music rather than just hearing it.

1. Say SOMETHING – you may get something right. But if you say nothing you will certainly get nothing right.

2. If you can't remember the Italian word, say it in English.

3. The questions you will be asked usually require only one-word or very short answers.

4. If you are a woodwind player, you may prefer to use the word "tongued" instead of detached (*staccato*).

5. Don't worry too much about complicated-sounding phrases like "articulation". The examiner will use words like "detached" and "smooth".

# FIND OUT THE MEANING

◁———— - gradually getting louder (*crescendo*)
————▷ - gradually getting quieter (*diminuendo*)
> - accent

⌒ - slur. Notes within a slur should be smooth.

*Accelerando, stringendo* – gradually getting faster
*Allegretto* – moderately quickly
*Andante* – at a walking speed
*Articulation* – how the notes are played or sung (smoothly or detached)
*Beat* – a unit of time. In 4/4 time there are four crotchet beats in a bar. Sometimes the word "pulse" is used for "beat"
*Compound time* – when the beat is divided into three; for example, in 6/8 there are two dotted-crotchet beats in a bar
*Crescendo, cresc.* – gradually getting louder
*Diminuendo, dim.* – gradually getting quieter
*Dynamics* – how loudly or quietly the notes are played or sung
*Forte, f* – loud
*Key* – major or minor. It also applies to the sharps (♯) or flats (♭) in the key signature. 'Sing in key' means sing in tune.
*Key-chord* – first, third and fifth notes of the scale
*Key note, tonic* – first note of the scale, or home note
*Largo* – slowly and broadly
*Legato* – smooth
*Melody, melodic* – tune
*Piano, p* – quiet, soft
*Pitch* – how high or low a note is
*Rallentando, ritardando* – gradually getting slower
*Rhythm* – notes of varying length grouped into patterns
*Staccato* – detached
*Tonality* – major or minor
*Tonic* – see *Key note*.

**Note:** The words used to introduce the tests may be slightly different to those used in this book.

*Answers to quiz questions:*
Page 9: 1 – 2-time; 2 – 4-time

Page 15: 1 – ⌐\⌐\    2 – ⌐\